CAN YOU FIND THE KNIGHTS TEMPLAR TREASURE?

AN INTERACTIVE TREASURE ADVENTURE
BY MATTHEW K. MANNING

CAPSTONE PRESS
a capstone imprint

Published by Capstone Press, an imprint of Capstone
1710 Roe Crest Drive
North Mankato, Minnesota 56003
capstonepub.com

Library of Congress Cataloging-in-Publication Data is
available on the Library of Congress website.
ISBN 9781669032052 (library binding)
ISBN 9781669032021 (paperback)
ISBN 9781669032038 (ebook PDF)

Summary: You've studied the history of the Knights Templar for years. The
mysterious order of religious warriors had great power and wealth in Europe in
the 1100s. But in the 1300s, the Templar order was scattered. Nobody knows what
happened to the knights' secrets or the gold and artifacts they may have left behind.
Now it's up to you to find out! Will the choices YOU make lead you to find the
Knights Templar lost treasure, or lead you to disaster?

Editorial Credits
Editor: Aaron Sautter; Designer: Bobbie Nuytten; Media Researcher:
Rebekah Hubstenberger; Production Specialist: Whitney Schaefer

Photo Credits
Alamy: Vincent Lowe, 44; Dreamstime: Catalin Iliescu, 12; Getty Images:
duncan1890, 9, iStock/Nachteule, 20, iStock/Valerio Bonaretti, 103, LordRunar,
cover, 1 (background), PATSTOCK, 96, Peter Zelei Images, 76, Westend61, 73,
ZU_09, 6, 41; Shutterstock: Alexander Khitrov, 83, andreonegin, 67, Andrey_
Kuzmin, design element (map), 1, Artem Kniaz, 60, Erika_Mondlova, 54, Fer
Gregory, cover (chest), IG Digital Arts, 36, Istomina Olena, 39, Misty River, 24,
Morphart Creation, 100, Net Vector, design element (light), Nielskliim, 79, Paul
Juser, 49, 53, Porcupen, 106-107, Vladimir Mulder, 27, 93

All internet sites appearing in back matter were available and accurate when this
book was sent to press.

TABLE OF CONTENTS

ABOUT YOUR ADVENTURE

YOU are a modern-day treasure hunter. You are hunting for the legendary treasure of the Knights Templar. This ancient religious society collected great wealth over the years. It is your dream to discover those hidden treasures.

Will you find ancient relics like the Holy Grail, or huge piles of gold? Or will you fall victim to deadly traps created centuries ago? YOU must decide where to search for the lost secrets of the Knights Templar. But be careful! One wrong step may leave you buried with the treasure you seek.

Chapter One sets the scene. Then you choose which path to read. Follow the directions at the bottom of the page as you read the stories. The decisions you make determine what happens next. After you finish one path, go back and read the others for new perspectives and more adventures.

Turn the page to begin your adventure.

The Knights Templar were active
across Europe from 1119 to 1312 CE.

CHAPTER 1

THE KNIGHTS OF LEGEND

All your years of study have led to this day. You've dedicated your life to learning about the crusading warrior monks known as the Knights Templar. You have long been fascinated by their history. And today, you'll put that knowledge to good use.

The Knights Templar were founded in the year 1119. They swore to the Catholic Church to remain poor and loyal, and to obey its teachings. These knights were originally charged with protecting pilgrims traveling to holy lands. Both Christians and Muslims claimed these lands as their holy birthright. As a result, many violent conflicts arose over these locations.

Turn the page.

As time passed, the Knights Templar grew more powerful. They fought many battles in various parts of the world. While they won and lost cities, they gained a heroic reputation. Kings relied on their forces. Common people looked to them as holy warriors.

Soon the rich and powerful began trusting their fortunes to the Templars' care. This allowed the Templars to act similarly to a bank. While traveling, people could leave their money with one group of Knights Templar. Then when they reached their destination, they could take out their fortune with a local group of Templars.

The Templars also lent money to many. Several kings fell into debt with the Templars, which gave them great political influence. Possessing so much wealth and power, the Templars seemed to disregard their oath to remain poor and humble.

The Knights Templar fought in many battles during religious wars known as the Crusades.

Turn the page.

When France's King Philip IV fell into debt with the Templars, he took matters into his own hands. He put the Templars on trial for sins they supposedly committed during their secretive ceremonies. Most people believed these claims were complete lies. But the king had great authority. So, the Templars were rounded up and either imprisoned or killed.

You've spent your life learning about the gold, valuables, and holy artifacts the Knights Templar could have guarded. In Scotland, the Rosslyn Chapel is rumored to have sheltered surviving members of the Templars. Perhaps the key to their treasure is hidden there.

Some believe that the Templars fled to North America and hid their treasures in New England. Still others think the Templars made their way to Bornholm, Denmark. Certain churches and markers there seem to hint at the Templars' fate.

Dangers lurk around every corner. Rumors even say that secret societies still work to keep the Templars' secrets to this day. The choice you make may leave you as doomed as the Templars themselves.

To begin your hunt in Scotland, turn to page 13.

To follow rumors to New England, turn to page 45.

To head to the small island called Bornholm, turn to page 73.

Rosslyn Chapel is located in the small town of Roslin south of Edinburgh, Scotland.

CHAPTER 2

THE SCOTTISH CONNECTION

You squint as you walk out of your hotel and into the morning sun. You feel a bit jet-lagged from your long flight from New York City. It doesn't help that here in Darvel, Scotland, it's five hours ahead of New York. You had terrible trouble getting to sleep last night. But you've traveled the world in search of the lost treasure of the Knights Templar. You'll adjust soon enough.

Across the street, your car is parked near a pub called the Lion's Head Tavern. It looks like a good place for dinner tonight. But right now, you have to go to an appointment at Rosslyn Chapel. It'll take you more than an hour to drive there.

Turn the page.

When you finally arrive at the chapel, it's every bit as impressive as you'd hoped. The castle-like chapel was built in 1446 and founded by Sir William St Clair. It is said to have ties to the Knights Templar due to its connection to William's grandfather, Henry Sinclair.

Some believe that surviving Templars hid in this very church after fleeing from King Philip IV. Rumors also say that Henry Sinclair may have traveled to North America long before Christopher Columbus.

"You're nearly late," says a voice from behind you. You turn to find an old woman, perhaps in her nineties. She's small, wears a bulky brown coat, and has a booming voice. "Let's get on with it."

You quickly realize that this old woman is the main caretaker of Rosslyn Chapel. When you were contacted by her assistant, you were warned about her no-nonsense personality.

You do your best to keep up as she heads into the visitor center outside the chapel. She waves at the young man taking tickets at the admissions counter. He nods knowingly and lets the two of you pass without paying.

Finally, you step inside the chapel. It is absolutely beautiful. Detailed carvings cover the walls and ceilings. Bright stained glass windows light the main chamber. You walk slowly between the rows of pews, taking it all in.

"No gawking!" says the old woman. "Keep up! Keep up!"

You hurry behind her until she stops in front of some temporary scaffolding.

"Up there," she grunts. She points to a rickety metal ladder. "Go on. I don't have all day."

You shrug and then climb the ladder and step onto the wobbly platform.

Turn the page.

From there, you can see a small hole in the stone wall. But the hole isn't cut out of stone. This small part of the wall is made of wood that was painted to look like stone.

You lean forward to look inside. There, at the back of the hole, is an engraved cross. It looks exactly like the symbol that the Knights Templar wore on their uniforms. Below the cross is an inscription written in French.

The engraving roughly translates to say, "Find the worthy lion."

You take a quick picture with your phone. Then you climb back down the wobbly ladder.

"They found that spot by accident when they were fixing the stonework," says the old woman. "You have any idea what it means?"

You immediately think of the gargoyles you saw outside the chapel. You remember thinking that they resemble lions. Could they be a clue to the treasure?

Then you think of the Lion's Head Tavern across the street from your hotel in Darvel. The tavern is old enough that it might still hold some secret Templar history. The entire town of Darvel sits on land once owned by the Templars, after all. That's the main reason you decided to stay there.

"Well?" asks the caretaker. "What do you think?"

To inspect the lion gargoyles, turn to page 18.
To head back to Darvel, turn to page 20.

You pull the ladder free from the scaffolding and rush outside with it. The old woman has trouble keeping up with you.

"You think the gargoyles are connected?" she asks. She suddenly looks excited.

"Yes, it's possible," you say. "The inscription says to 'Find the worthy lion.' The gargoyles look a lot like lions, don't you think?"

You lean the ladder against an outer wall in the chapel's courtyard. Then you scurry up its rungs. You examine one of the strange lion-like gargoyles. Its stone mouth hangs open to let rainwater drain from the church's roof. There's nothing unusual about this gargoyle. You climb back down the ladder and move it over a few feet to inspect the next lion gargoyle.

You repeat your search until you've looked at every gargoyle.

"How long is this gonna take?" asks the old woman. The excitement has long since faded from her face.

"I have it narrowed down to two," you say. "But we've got to be careful. We could stumble on some sort of ancient booby trap."

"Which two?" she asks.

"The one on the far corner, and the third lion there," you say, pointing to each. "Each one has a marking on its back. The one down there has a cross. And this one here has an X."

"Does it really? Well now, that's something. What now?" the old woman asks.

To pick the lion with the cross, turn to page 22.
To choose the lion with the 'X,' turn to page 24.

Before you came to Scotland, you heard a lot about the small town of Darvel. The lands the town rests on once belonged to the Knights Templar. If the treasure of the Knights Templar exists, it might be hidden somewhere in Darvel.

You jump in your rental car and speed back to where you started the day. On the way, you admire the rolling green hills of the Scottish countryside.

About an hour later, you're standing outside the Lion's Head Tavern. You turn back to the front door of the pub and walk in.

It's darker inside than you expected. When your eyes adjust, you see a couple in the corner of the room eating some sort of stew. A bartender is munching on a sandwich behind the bar. You nod to him. He doesn't respond. He doesn't seem too friendly.

You see a hall leading toward the back of the tavern. At the end of the hall, you see a large lion's head painted on the wall.

You look back at the bartender. He's still staring at you. You could head straight down the hall to check out the painted lion's head. But maybe you should talk to the bartender first.

To talk with the bartender, turn to page 31.
To head to the hallway, turn to page 33.

The Knights Templar wore uniforms with famous red crosses on their chests. Knowing that makes the choice easy. You move the ladder under the lion with the cross on its back. Then you climb the ladder to inspect the lion gargoyle more closely.

You place your hand near the gargoyle and a spider skitters out from under your fingers. You jerk your hand back in surprise. But the spider suddenly becomes more interesting than creepy. Because as you watch it, the spider slips under a claw on the gargoyle's back right paw.

When you examine the paw more carefully, you notice that only this one claw is raised higher than the others. You try to push the claw. It doesn't budge. Then you reach into your pocket and pull out your car keys. Carefully, you slip the end of one key underneath the claw. You pull the claw backward.

RRMMMMBBBLLL!

You suddenly feel the ground tremble beneath your feet. You practically slide down the ladder. Then you sprint to the opposite side of the chapel where the rumbling seemed the loudest. A large, flat stone in the walkway has slid open. Beneath it is an old stone staircase. Dust and spiderwebs decorate the steps. It looks as though no one has used them for centuries.

"What in the world?" the caretaker exclaims as she joins you by the steps.

You pull out your phone and tap on its flashlight.

"Oh no you don't," says the woman. "There could be all kinds of old traps down there. We'd best call the authorities and wait."

To explore the stone stairs anyway, turn to page 26.

To wait for the authorities to arrive, turn to page 29.

All your life, you've heard that 'X' marks the spot. It seems too simple, but the gargoyle with the 'X' on its back seems like the best choice.

You move the ladder and climb up to the lion with the 'X.' After looking it over for a few minutes, you notice the lion's mane seems to be carved with less detail than the rest of its body.

A carved head of a lion at Rosslyn Chapel

"Find the worthy lion," you say to yourself. You place your hand on the back of the gargoyle's head. Then you simply pet the lion, as if it were a house cat. You feel the stone mane shift under your palm.

The mane lowers slightly, and then you hear a rumbling sound. You look up just in time to see the roof of the chapel slide toward you. You try to climb down the ladder, but you're not fast enough. The entire roof of the church has slid off the stone walls and on to you.

The caretaker lets out a cry of shock as you're buried under an avalanche of stone and wood. It's the last sound you ever hear.

THE END

To follow another path, turn to page 11.
To learn more about the Knights Templar,
turn to page 101.

You didn't come all the way to Scotland to turn back at the first sign of danger.

"Sorry," you say to the caretaker. "I won't be long."

You slowly step onto the first stone stair, then the next. A large roach scurries out of the way of your shoe. But you hardly notice. You're too busy looking at the many carvings of crosses and ancient runes along the walls.

At the bottom of the stairs, you shine your phone's light ahead of you. The tunnel ends only five or six feet ahead at a wall made of large stone bricks. You walk over to it and explore its slick, slightly damp surface with your fingers.

Then one of the stones in the wall gives way. It slides inward. The stone brick topples to the ground behind the wall. Then the others begin to crumble and slide out of place.

Ancient castles and buildings in Europe often have secret chambers and passages hidden inside.

You leap back for safety, but the stone bricks all fall in the opposite direction. They cave in, forming a perfect doorway where the wall once stood.

Turn the page.

You step over the fallen rocks and into a large chamber. You shine your light ahead of you, but a reflection momentarily blinds you. Your eyes soon adjust, but you can't believe what you see.

In front of you are piles and piles of ancient gold coins and solid gold bars. After only one day in Scotland, you've successfully discovered the treasure of the Knights Templar! You can't wait to see the look on the old caretaker's face.

THE END

To follow another path, turn to page 11.
To learn more about the Knights Templar,
turn to page 101.

You have made a career out of being careful. So you decide to curb your excitement for a little longer and listen to the caretaker's advice.

"I don't see the harm in waiting a bit," you say.

"Wise man," says the old woman. She walks away from you and pulls a phone from her pocket. She appears to dial a number, then smiles over at you.

After ten minutes, you grow impatient and walk toward the caretaker. She raises a finger, as if she's still talking on the phone. Then you hear a rumbling behind you.

You spin around just in time to see the stone panel sliding shut once more.

"We waited too long!" you shout.

You race around the chapel and quickly climb back up the ladder.

Turn the page.

At the top, you slide your key under the lion's claw again, but it won't budge. You keep trying, and the claw breaks off. Whatever ancient mechanism it triggered before wasn't built to work twice.

As you head back down the ladder, you find the caretaker waiting for you. She has a smile on her face. "Well, I guess some things just aren't meant to be," she says.

She waves at you and heads back inside Rosslyn Chapel. For the first time, you notice a large ring on her hand. On that ring is the red cross of the Knights Templar. Despite what the history books say, it seems the organization is still alive and well. And they're just as secretive as ever.

THE END

To follow another path, turn to page 11.
To learn more about the Knights Templar,
turn to page 101.

You can't avoid the bartender for long. You figure you might as well talk to him and see what he has to say.

"Hello," you say, taking a seat on one of the circular stools at the bar.

"Hmm," the bartender grunts.

"I was wondering if you might know any of the history of this place," you say. "The stone walls look pretty old."

"Hmm," he grunts again. Then he walks to the other end of the bar. He picks up his phone from the counter. He's far enough away that you can't hear his conversation.

After a few minutes, the front door to the tavern swings open. Two police officers stand in the doorway, lit by the bright sun behind them.

"You there," one says, pointing in your direction. "Come with us."

Turn the page.

You follow them outside. "What's this all about?" you ask.

As they help you into their squad car, one of the officers says, "You've been asking the wrong type of questions, son. Some powerful people would rather you didn't."

Whatever secret the Lion's Head Tavern is hiding will remain a secret. At least until you can talk your way out of a jail cell.

THE END

To follow another path, turn to page 11.
To learn more about the Knights Templar,
turn to page 101.

You pretend not to notice the bartender's glare as you walk toward the back hallway. The couple in the corner watches you pass by. If there's any other entertainment in this small town, you wouldn't know about it. Everyone seems perfectly happy just to watch you.

You walk past a door to the kitchen and the door to the restrooms.

At the end of the hall, you examine the large lion head. Above it are the words, "To the worthy goes the world."

"Find the worthy lion," you say to yourself, thinking of the inscription at the chapel.

You touch the lion's head with your palm. To your surprise, your hand passes right through it. The lion's head wasn't painted on a wall at all. It was painted on a thin piece of material, a linen curtain tacked into place.

Turn the page.

You push the hanging cloth to the side. Behind it is a hole in the wall about the size of a window. You glance over your shoulder to see if anyone is watching. There's no one in sight. So you climb through the open window into a secret chamber. This part of the old building is certainly not meant for visitors!

In front of you are two dark, crudely carved tunnels. You hear footsteps in the pub behind you. You need to make a choice—fast.

To take the tunnel to the left, go to page 35.

To take the tunnel to the right, turn to page 38.

You have no time to think about it. You sprint down the tunnel to your left. But it's so dark you can barely see where you're going. All you can do is keep your arms outstretched in front of you to make sure you don't run into anything.

Behind you, the faint sound of footsteps grows louder.

Suddenly, you slam into something hard. You reach out and feel around with your hands. The object in front of you is cold, like metal. Then you find a ring-shaped handle. You grab hold of it and pull, and the metal door opens. You rush inside and slam the door behind you.

Pulling your phone from your pocket, you tap on its flashlight. Then you gasp. In front of you is a human skeleton! Its hands are chained to the jagged rock wall behind it. On its chest is a torn shirt. The material is rotten with age. Still, you recognize the red cross of the Knights Templar.

Turn the page.

Dark castle dungeons were often used to imprison enemies and torture them for information.

You shine your phone's light around the rest of the small chamber. It appears to be a medieval dungeon. There's nothing in the room but a small metal cage and a pail in the corner.

You realize your only choice is to head back through the steel door. But when you try the handle, it doesn't budge. It's locked! You try to call for help on your phone, but there's no signal down here.

"Help!" you shout through the door. There's no answer. You try the door again. It still doesn't open. "Help!" you shout again.

You hold your breath to listen. You can hear a faint sound from the other side of the door. But it's the sound of laughter. With horror, you realize that you'll never leave this chamber again.

THE END

To follow another path, turn to page 11.
To learn more about the Knights Templar,
turn to page 101.

You turn and race down the tunnel to the right. You know you have a minute or two at most before the bartender catches up to you. You need to move as fast as you can if you're going to find any secrets hidden in this place.

The passageway is so dark it's hard to see. But that changes as soon as you turn a corner. Surprisingly, there are lit candles lining the walls. They flicker as you pass them, held in place by antique fixtures.

Behind you, the footsteps grow louder. You're sure it's the bartender. And he's much bigger than you are. Ignoring the burning in your lungs, you pick up speed and run as fast as you can. You turn another corner and nearly run smack into a stone lion's head carved into the tunnel itself.

"Find the worthy lion," you say between hard breathing. You trace your hand over the lion's face. The footsteps sound louder behind you.

Then your hand comes to a stop over the lion's left eye. There, barely visible, is a proper Templar cross, carved right into the big cat's pupil.

"I've got you trapped now!" yells the bartender from around the corner.

You press the eye. The sound of rumbling rock fills the tunnel. The lion's head seems to turn sideways, as if getting a better look at you.

Turn the page.

Then you realize that the carving is turning. As it rolls sideways, it reveals a circle-shaped doorway in the wall. Soon enough, the hole is large enough to fit through. You squeeze into the chamber behind it. And just as quickly, the large lion head snaps back into place.

"Hey!" you hear the bartender call from the other side of the wall. "Where'd ya go?"

You try to breathe as quietly as possible as you tap on your phone's flashlight.

In front of you is a chamber as beautifully decorated as the Rosslyn Chapel. Every inch of the wall is covered in detailed carvings. It reads like a visual history of the Knights Templar.

You see a carving of a building, which you recognize as the legendary Temple of Solomon. It was rumored that the Templars explored the fallen temple to recover lost religious artifacts.

You look at a carving of a knight standing outside the temple. He is holding a simple drinking cup. It must be the legendary Holy Grail!

According to Christian history, the Holy Grail was believed to be the cup used by Jesus Christ at the famous Last Supper before he was crucified.

Turn the page.

Looking to the right, you see a detailed, life-size statue of a knight. In his hand is a cup. You reach for it. It easily pulls away from the statue. From your years of study, you are certain that this is the real, genuine Holy Grail.

Suddenly, the chamber begins to shake. Removing the Holy Grail has triggered some ancient device. You look up to see a panel in the ceiling sliding open. Sunlight fills the chamber. You see the bottom rung of a wooden ladder just above your head. You can't go back to the bar now. So, you slip the Grail into your jacket and jump for the ladder.

The first rung breaks away in your hands. But you try again. You manage to grab ahold of both sides of the ladder. You pull yourself up and grab a higher rung. It holds. You climb and don't stop until you emerge from a well in the middle of a bright green field.

Beneath you, you can see the stone panel sliding back into place. The secret chamber is hidden once more. But in your jacket pocket is the Holy Grail.

You look across the small field at the back of the Lion's Head Tavern. You must have traveled at least two city blocks in those underground tunnels! You hurry back past the bar and to your hotel. You'll leave for New York City in the morning. And with you, you'll take the greatest discovery of your life.

THE END

To follow another path, turn to page 11.
To learn more about the Knights Templar,
turn to page 101.

A statue of Henry Sinclair in Scotland shows him holding a shield with the cross engraved on it.

CHAPTER 3

THE NEW WORLD

Even as you walk through the airport at Providence, Rhode Island, you're not sure exactly what you're doing here. You're determined to follow every clue about the Knights Templar treasure. But you have doubts that the treasure might be here in New England.

For hundreds of years, rumors have said that Scottish nobleman Henry Sinclair had strong ties to the Knights Templar. He may have even been a member.

Supposedly, some ancient letters indicated that Sinclair was an explorer and discovered North America long before Christopher Columbus. But most historians doubt it happened.

Turn the page.

The Knights Templar were forced to disband long before Sinclair was born. However, some researchers believe that the Knights Templar were so powerful that King Philip IV couldn't have shut them down completely. They think that a few of the Templars survived and hid their greatest treasures and secrets. It's possible that the treasures were first smuggled to Scotland and then brought to North America.

You shrug as you pick up the rental car you reserved. Despite your doubts, if there's any possibility that Sinclair traveled from Scotland to the New World, then he may have brought the Knights Templar treasure with him.

Most experts say these theories lack historical proof. But if Henry Sinclair did explore North America, it's thought he first visited Nova Scotia in Canada. Then he continued to Rhode Island and Massachusetts.

You've narrowed your choices down to two areas of interest. But you haven't quite decided which one to explore.

In Newport, Rhode Island, stands the Newport Tower. Rumors say that the ancient structure could have been built by Henry Sinclair and the Knights Templar. In Westford, Massachusetts, there is a carving of what appears to be a Templar Knight. This suggests that Sinclair might have traveled to that location as well. Either place could provide clues to the treasure of the Knights Templar.

Even after coming all this way, you're not sure where to start. You sit in your car and think it over. You only have enough time to visit one of these sites.

To drive to the Newport Tower,
turn to page 48.

To head to Westford, Massachusetts,
turn to page 52.

It comes down to which location is closer. Newport, Rhode Island, is only a forty-minute drive away. You decide to check out the Newport Tower. When you arrive and park your car in Newport, you're greeted by a cool afternoon breeze.

You see the tower right away. It's a large cylinder made of stacked stones of different shapes and sizes. At its base are a series of archways on top of eight columns. You're struck by how similar the structure is to some round churches in Europe.

You walk through the gate of the spiked metal fence that surrounds the tower. Looking up, you see blue sky through the open top where a roof once sat. The tower is clearly made of tons of ancient stones. But one in particular soon catches your eye.

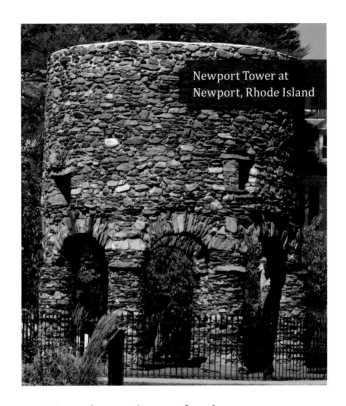
Newport Tower at
Newport, Rhode Island

Near the top layer of rocks, you spot a
small indentation on a large stone. It's too
high to reach. So you pull out the pair of travel
binoculars that you keep in your shoulder bag.
You use them to get a closer look at the stone.
The marking appears to be an upside-down 'V.'
Or maybe it's something else entirely. Maybe the
point of the 'V' is actually an arrow.

Turn the page.

You look past the structure and see an empty grassy corner of the park. With houses and businesses nearby, it seems odd that this plot of land is undisturbed.

You reach into your bag and pull out your notebook. You flip through your notes on the Newport Tower until you find a photo you copied from an old book at your local library. It clearly shows the Newport Tower. Behind the tower is a large oak tree. A tree that once sat on that same empty plot of land.

"Looking for something?" asks a shaky voice from your left. You turn to see a skinny bald man. "Perhaps an oak tree?" he asks.

The man is the curator at the Newport Tower's nearby museum. He welcomes you inside and walks you to an exhibit in the corner of the room. There on the wall is a photo of the oak tree. A flat stone rests in a glass case below the picture.

"When we had to cut down that old oak, they found that stone buried beneath its roots," says the curator. He removes the stone from its case to give you a better look. "Curious thing. Looks almost like a map."

"It does," you say. You pull out your phone and compare the stone to a current road map.

Using the Newport Tower as a starting point, the stone map seems to lead to a local dock. Then a thought occurs to you, and you ask the curator to turn the stone upside down. Viewed this way, the map seems to lead to a nearby cemetery.

"Huh," says the curator. "Would you look at that! Seems like you have a choice, son."

To head to the dock, turn to page 57.
To go to the cemetery, turn to page 59.

Even though the trip is longer, you think the carving in Westford, Massachusetts, has more potential. You'd like to examine the Westford Knight with your own eyes. When you arrive in Westford, you pass by a gift shop that seems to specialize in all things medieval.

"I must be in the right place," you say to yourself.

You park your car at a nearby high school and walk to what looks like a natural rock formation. In the rock is the faint image of a knight with a sword and a shield. The knight's form is barely visible. It seems to have been worn away by the elements over hundreds of years.

What strikes you right away is that the angle of the sword is odd. It doesn't look as perfectly placed as other Templar artifacts you've seen. It's almost as if the blade of the sword is a marker pointing to something in the distance.

A bronze sculpture of the Westford Knight was placed near the rock carving in 2015.

"You know, if you want more info about that old thing, you might try the Masonic Temple down the street," says an old man from a nearby path. "Those fellas really know their stuff when it comes to this old secret business."

To follow where the sword is pointing, turn to page 54.

To visit the Masonic Temple, turn to page 62.

Something about this old man seems off. You're not sure what it is, and you'd rather not stick around to find out. You quickly thank him for the advice, then head off in the direction that the carved sword is pointing.

After walking a bit, you chance upon a small stream. Over it stands a stone bridge. It appears ancient. It may be as old as the slab of rock that contains the Westford Knight.

You follow the stream under the bridge and look carefully at the stone bricks that make up the old structure. Between two of them is a strange-looking slot. It's about three inches wide.

You move closer to get a good look at the slot in the stones. It looks about the same width as the sword in the Westford Knight carving. Then you remember the small gift shop you passed by earlier. You immediately know what you must do. You sprint toward your car as fast as you can.

Twenty minutes later, you're back under the stone bridge. In your hand, you hold a souvenir sword. Its blade is dull, but it should do the job. You approach the slot and slide the end of the blade into the stone.

It fits! The blade slides all the way into the slot until its handle hits stone.

Turn the page.

Then you hear a slight rumble, and your sword falls to the ground. The rocks on either side of the slot have shifted open, revealing a stone doorway. You walk inside and cough from the decades of dust that fill your lungs. The chamber is small and contains only one object. But it's an amazing find. You are looking at the Spear of Destiny!

According to Christian lore, this is the spear that pierced the side of Jesus Christ during his crucifixion. It is undoubtably the most valuable of all the Knights Templar treasures. You pick up the spear and can't help but think that Destiny is an appropriate name for what you've just discovered.

THE END

To follow another path, turn to page 11.
To learn more about the Knights Templar,
turn to page 101.

The sun has set by the time you arrive at the dock. There are a few old stone buildings near the water. You decide that you'll have to come back tomorrow to get a better look. If the stone is a map, then one of those houses is likely home to the treasure of the Knights Templar.

It seems too late in the day to bother the owners now, though. Instead, you stroll out to the end of a rickety wooden pier. It's a peaceful evening. You don't see another person anywhere around. You take a deep breath of the salty air.

"Turn around slowly," rasps a shaky voice.

You do as the voice commands. You turn to see the curator of the Newport Tower Museum. He has a gun in his hand—pointed right at you.

Turn the page.

"What's this about?" you ask.

"There are those of us still tasked with keeping the Templars' secrets," says the man. "And we're sworn to protect them from the likes of you."

You start to protest. But before saying anything, you hear a loud bang, and you slump to the ground. As you shut your eyes for the last time, at least you'll die knowing that the treasure is real.

THE END

To follow another path, turn to page 11.
To learn more about the Knights Templar,
turn to page 101.

You follow the stone map's markings to the Island Cemetery of Newport. The museum curator said that it's the oldest cemetery in Rhode Island. The site was originally given to the city in 1640. It already had a few modest headstones back then. Some of those graves might even be old enough to have been dug by Henry Sinclair and his men.

Judging by the stone map's crude engraving, the trail ends at an old mausoleum. The structure looks too modern to be made by the Templars, however.

Even so, you try the mausoleum's door. To your surprise, it opens easily. You walk inside the small room. There is a stone tomb at the center. An ancient stone serves as the grave's lid. It appears much older than the entire mausoleum.

"I've come this far," you say to yourself. "Might as well see this through."

Turn the page.

You slide the lid to the side. Inside the tomb, there is no skeleton. There's no body of any sort. Instead, there's a stone staircase. You take a deep breath and steady your nerves. Then you step into the tomb and walk down the stairs.

When you reach the bottom, it's pitch black. You pull your flashlight from your bag and shine it in front of you. But you're not prepared for what you see. You're not in some small tunnel. You've stumbled into a huge cavern. Even more fascinating, this giant chamber seems to house an old, run-down ghost town.

There are several buildings in front of you built right into the cavern wall! One looks like a church. Another looks like an old trader's shop. A third building appears to have had its roof and walls cave in. You've never seen anything like this before. You certainly don't want to stop exploring now.

To head into the church, turn to page 64.

To explore the shop, turn to page 66.

Many legends tie the Knights Templar to the modern secret society called the Free and Accepted Masons. Each group of Freemasons was charged with many secrets and made up of powerful members of the ruling class. Even much of the imagery of the two groups is remarkably similar.

You thank the old man for the advice and walk in the direction he pointed to find the Masonic Temple. The walk takes a bit longer than you expected. When you make a final turn, you realize you're in a dead-end alleyway.

"Lost, stranger?" says a large man standing behind you. On either side of him is another equally intimidating bruiser. It seems the old man has led you into a trap.

The three large men walk toward you. They don't seem like they want a friendly chat. You take your bag off your shoulder and hurl it at the man in the center.

Surprised, he fumbles to hold onto it. In that split second, you bolt past him. You run as fast as you can for as long as you can. When you finally stop, you realize that the men didn't follow you.

However, you have no idea what your next move should be. Should you tell the authorities and risk alerting others to your search? Or should you try to find the Masonic Temple on your own?

To head to the local police station, turn to page 69.

To try to find the Masonic Temple, turn to page 70.

You think the logical place to hide the Knights Templar treasure would be in the underground church. You walk through its large double doors and into the main chamber. Dusty pews line the aisle. A few of these pews have fallen over. The dust is so thick on the stone floor, it's more like dirt. You leave footprints behind you as you walk. You approach the altar. On it, you see an old, worn cup.

This is it, you think. *I actually found it!*

There is no doubt in your mind. You believe you've found the cup Jesus drank from during the Last Supper. You've discovered the Holy Grail of Christian lore.

But when you lift the cup off the altar, you discover that it's attached to a cord. The cup feels wooden, cheap, and hollow. And by pulling its cord, you've triggered something.

As soon as you realize this is a trap, the ceiling begins to crumble above you. Large chunks of stone and wood rain down onto the floor. You sprint for the front door but slip and fall thanks to the thick dust.

You found an underground village when you climbed into the tomb. But in the end, you're just another body buried at the cemetery.

THE END

To follow another path, turn to page 11.
To learn more about the Knights Templar,
turn to page 101.

It might make sense that the Knights Templar would hide their valuables in a church. But from your experience, treasure is never hidden in the obvious place. Instead, you decide to check inside the underground shop.

You're surprised by how old everything looks inside. There are glass jars topping many of the shelves. Whatever was inside them has long since molded or melted.

Along with the jars are rows of old, unlabeled bottles. There are also pouches of mysterious powders. And rows of books and scrolls line the shelves that look like they could crumble with the slightest touch.

A counter separates the store from a back room. You walk behind the counter and into a large, empty space.

There is only one object in this room: a small chest. It is about the size of a shoebox. Its wooden lid is decorated with leather straps that have dried and nearly disintegrated with age.

You steady yourself and then slowly open the chest. Inside is a modest piece of wood. Yet it is decorated with rubies that flicker in the light of your flashlight.

Turn the page.

You recognize the object from the many descriptions you've read. This is a piece of the cross of Christ. It's a fragment of the most famous cross in Christian history. It is said that Jesus was crucified on this very wood. It is one of the most priceless artifacts in human history.

You have successfully unearthed the treasure of the Knights Templar. And it is more spectacular than you had ever dreamed possible.

THE END

To follow another path, turn to page 11.
To learn more about the Knights Templar,
turn to page 101.

There's no sense in continuing your quest if you can't do it safely. So you head to the nearest police station and report the three men from the alleyway.

"Hmm," says the officer behind the front desk. "That *is* serious. Better follow me."

You do as he says, and he leads you into a holding cell.

"Sounds like you were seeing things that you shouldn't," he says. Then he smiles. "Maybe you'll realize you were imagining things after spending a week or two in here," he says, walking away.

Apparently, the secrets of the Knights Templar go beyond what the history books say. The people of this town will never let you discover the truth.

THE END

To follow another path, turn to page 11.
To learn more about the Knights Templar,
turn to page 101.

It takes a bit of poking around, but you finally discover an old building. The words "Masonic Temple" are carved above its large double doors. The building is nowhere near where the old man told you to go. This town seems to be full of secrets.

You knock on the door, and no one answers. So you pull the handle and step inside. Opposite you, a large red Templar cross is painted on a white wall. There is a door on either side of the empty room. As you think about which one to investigate, you hear a familiar voice behind you.

"Hello again," he says.

The same men from the alleyway are blocking the entrance to the building. You begin to back away and bump into the wall behind you.

"Our order doesn't permit visitors," says the large man. "And trespassers are punished."

You sprint toward the door to your left, but the men beat you to it. They tackle you and drag you to the ground.

"Long live the Templar!" one of them says, raising his fist. Those are the last words you'll ever hear.

THE END

To follow another path, turn to page 11.
To learn more about the Knights Templar, turn to page 101.

Hammershus Fortress overlooks the sea from a hilltop on the coast of Bornholm, Denmark.

CHAPTER 4

THE MYSTERY ISLAND

The wind whips through your jacket as you stand on a hill in Bornholm, Denmark. There aren't many in the United States who know of this tiny Scandinavian island. But the mysteries it offers are too tempting to resist.

"Glad to see you've arrived," a young man with blond hair calls from across a bright green patch of land. He walks over to you with his hand extended. You shake it, but aren't sure who you're meeting. You haven't told anyone you were coming here.

"The name's Henry," he says. "I'm your guide."

"I think there's been some mistake," you say. "I haven't arranged for a tour guide."

Turn the page.

"Nonsense," he says. "Someone of your reputation doesn't need to ask for a tour. You get one for free!"

"But how did you know I was going to be—"

"Up ahead are some of the many standing stones on our island," he interrupts. He gestures toward a few large rocks jutting up from the ground near the shore. "I imagine that's what you've come to see."

"Not in particular," you say. "I was actually interested in some churches."

You've heard of the standing stones that mysteriously dot Bornholm. But the main reason you came is to see four circular churches. The churches seem to mimic several Knights Templar churches in Europe. If the Templars journeyed to Bornholm centuries ago, then the churches might lead you to their lost treasures.

"Oh, tourists come here all the time to look at our churches," Henry says. "But they've been picked over by anyone with the tiniest curiosity. I know you're a true expert. You don't want to see the tourist spots. You need to see the real deal."

With that, he gives you a huge grin. It looks like he has more teeth than he should. Despite seeming a little strange, Henry makes a good point. You could go with him or decide to seek out the treasure on your own.

To inspect the standing stones with Henry, turn to page 76.

To visit a church alone, turn to page 79.

You decide it might be best to see Bornholm from a local citizen's point of view. So you follow Henry toward the shore. There, in the middle of a patch of trees, stand two large stones. They're as big as boulders, and they've been placed to stand up on end.

Several hundred mysterious standing stones are scattered around the island of Bornholm.

No natural rock formation sticks straight up from the ground like that. You're sure that they were put there by people. The question is, when?

"Our standing stones used to decorate the island in the thousands. Now there are only a few hundred of them left," Henry tells you. "But I wanted you to see these two in particular. They date back to around 3000 BCE, but they seem to have been altered centuries later."

When you get close enough, you realize what Henry means. Each of the stones has crude carvings on them. They appear to each bear the unique cross of the Knights Templar. The only difference is that the stone on the left is unfinished. The carver didn't bother to connect the bottom side of the cross.

"I can't believe these are out here in plain sight like this," you say under your breath.

Turn the page.

You've heard legends about standing stones blocking the entrance to underground tunnels. These two look very similar to the ones described in an old book you discovered a few years ago.

Your thoughts are interrupted by the ringing of Henry's phone. "Sorry," he says. "I've got to take this."

He turns his back to you and begins to walk away. If you're going to act and uncover an ancient tunnel, you need to do it now.

To move the stone with the unfinished cross, turn to page 82.

To move the stone with the finished cross, turn to page 84.

Something about Henry seems strange to you. So you turn down his offer and set off on your own toward one of Bornholm's four circular churches.

You're happy with your choice. The church is impressive. Several other visitors are exploring the church grounds too. You walk around outside the building to take it all in. The church contains several levels. You can see many narrow windows cut into its ancient stone wall.

Several ancient round churches are found on the island of Bornholm.

Turn the page.

You head inside and notice that the original church was built around a column. There are large archways in the column, allowing you to walk right into the church's hollow center.

The only buildings you've ever seen like this church were constructed by the Knights Templar. This building is strangely close in design.

There is a row of uneven steps lining the wall. You follow them up in a spiral until you get to the next level. There are eight windows cut into the stone walls on this second floor. You remember reading that the windows seem designed to let light travel through the building during the first sunlight of the winter solstice. The design is much more advanced than other buildings of this era.

But as you look through one of the windows, you notice something else. You can see all the way through the church and the window on the opposite side.

But more than that, the top of a hill is framed perfectly in the center of your view. You wonder if this was a way of seeing enemies approaching. Or perhaps it means something more?

As you think on this, you continue to walk around this level of the church. You see another set of stone stairs. You hadn't realized there was a third level to the building.

You can see through another window that the sun is setting. You want to inspect the highest level of the church, but you also want to explore that nearby hilltop. It will soon be too dark to see both the rest of the church and the surrounding countryside.

To head to the hilltop, turn to page 86.
To finish exploring the church, turn to page 90.

When Henry disappears over a nearby grassy hill, you leap into action. You rush over to the standing stone with the unfinished cross. Using all your strength, you manage to push it over. Just as you guessed, beneath it is a stone stairway leading to an underground tunnel.

You smile and quickly hurry down the uneven staircase. You're sure Henry wouldn't approve of you disturbing a historical site like this. But if you're going to explore, this is your only chance.

Once at the base of the staircase, you pull out your phone and tap on its flashlight function. Then you shine it at the open chamber in front of you.

A long, crudely dug tunnel stretches out before you. You continue into it without thinking twice. This is exactly the kind of ancient secret you traveled to Bornholm to find.

It isn't long before you hear the sounds of
trickling water. Your nostrils fill with a foul odor.
You soon come upon a second tunnel that leads
to the right. You've clearly come upon a sewer
system of some sort. You're not sure whether
to continue on your current path or explore the
sewer. But you need to decide before Henry
catches up with you.

To explore the sewer, turn to page 92.
To continue down the tunnel, turn to page 94.

You choose the standing stone with the finished cross. It seems the most accurate to the drawings you've seen in your history books. Henry has walked over a hill and can neither hear nor see what you're doing. But you still need to be quick about it.

You lean against the large standing stone and push with all your might. The rock is nearly as tall as you are. It definitely weighs more than you do. But finally, it budges. The stone topples over with a thud.

You're shocked to see what lies beneath it. There is an opening in the ground about two feet by two feet wide. The hole looks like a crude tunnel carved through solid stone.

You notice that there are small ledges on one side of the stone hole. They look almost like the rungs of a ladder. Without a moment's pause, you climb down into the darkness.

When your shoe touches the bottom of the hole, you're surprised that there's no connecting tunnel. It's just a slim vertical shaft in the ground.

You look up and begin to climb toward daylight once again. But suddenly, the hole grows dark. Someone has moved the standing stone back into its former position!

You push against the new stone ceiling, but it doesn't budge. And it never will. The standing stone will soon become your own personal grave marker.

THE END

To follow another path, turn to page 11.
To learn more about the Knights Templar,
turn to page 101.

The hilltop is too tempting to ignore. So you head back down the stone stairs and out the church's main entrance.

Ten minutes later, you stand atop the grassy hill. To your surprise, the hill is actually a cliff. You look over its far end and see waves lapping against the base of a steep rock wall. It must be a good hundred feet to the sea from where you are standing.

Then you notice a small dirt path in the grass at your feet. It trails over the edge of the cliff. From there, a small ledge path clings to the cliffside. It's less than a foot wide.

Although the sun is setting, you're feeling excited and brave. You take a few steps down the narrow ledge. Then you press your body up against the rock face and scoot farther across the thin overhang.

It takes a half hour, but you make good progress. Eventually, you reach the ledge's end. There, a large rock juts out of the side of the cliff. It doesn't seem like you can go any farther.

But then you notice two indentations above your head in the rock. You might be able to use them as handholds. You look down at the waves below. Sharp rocks jut out of the water. The ocean seems to be getting rougher as the wind picks up. You take a deep breath. Then you stretch for the handholds.

You hold as tightly as you can and step off the ledge. With nothing left to stand on, your arms strain under your own weight. You look to your left and can now see around the large rock. There's a cave entrance just a few feet away. You gather all your strength. Then you fling yourself toward the cave's mouth.

Turn the page.

You land on your stomach on the ledge. It hurts, but you pull yourself up from there. A long, shadowy cave tunnel stretches out before you. You stand up, pull out your phone, and turn on the flashlight function. You set off into the darkness, using your phone to light the way.

At the end of the tunnel, you think you've gone as far as you can go. Then you see a large crack in the ceiling above you. You jump up and manage to pull yourself into it. You grip the stone wall and use your legs to kick yourself up. You can just barely squeeze through.

Once you're through, you take a look around. You realize you're in a higher section of the cave. You see an old treasure chest in the center of this otherwise empty chamber. The chest is wrapped in a white flag with a red Templar cross painted on it.

You get to your feet and pull the flag off the chest. The aged wood of the trunk splinters as you open it. There's a musty smell to the chest. It's as if the air has been sealed inside it for generations. Inside the chest sits a lone leather-bound book.

The corners of the book's pages crumble and flake off as you flip through it. You skim the text and quickly realize what you're reading. They are missing chapters of the Christian Bible. You've made an incredible discovery! But the book feels so fragile, you're not sure it will survive the climb back to the surface. You need to preserve it as best you can. But how?

To take the book and climb to the surface, turn to page 96.

To take pictures of the book with your phone, turn to page 98.

Since you're already at the church, it seems best to see the whole thing while you're here. So you head to the nearby steps and walk up to the highest level.

Once again, the stairs wrap around the structure in a spiral fashion. They're even more uneven on this level. You nearly lose your footing a time or two.

It's particularly hard to keep your balance when a young couple rushes by you. They're apparently in a hurry to leave the church. But finally, you reach the top. You open a heavy wooden door and walk into a tiny, circular room.

The setting sun's rays shoot through the narrow windows. You peer through one of these slots and are surprised to see no other people on the surrounding grounds. There were many other visitors when you first entered the church.

Suddenly, you hear footsteps coming up the stairs behind you. Then the door to your small room slams shut! You try the handle, but it won't budge. You pull out your phone to call for help, but when you do, you see that the battery is dead.

You scream for help, but no one comes. There's no one around to even hear you. You don't know who locked you in the chamber, but you feel the chill of the night creeping in. Your only hope is that someone finds you tomorrow morning. And that whoever locked you in here doesn't come back.

THE END

To follow another path, turn to page 11.
To learn more about the Knights Templar,
turn to page 101.

You do your best to ignore the smell and step into the sewer tunnel. Flowing through the tunnel is a wide river of muck and grime. Luckily, there's a two-foot ledge on either side. You stick to the ledge and slowly continue on.

You begin to pick up the pace a bit. You're excited to see what lies at the end of the tunnel. But you almost lose your balance when you hear Henry's voice behind you.

"In a hurry?" he asks.

You steady yourself and then shine your light at Henry. He gives you a wide smile. Then he shoves you!

There's no time to react. You fall deep into the muck of the sewer. You try to surface, but your coat snags on something in the dark sludge.

Underground sewer systems are found in many old cities and towns across Europe.

You furiously try to untangle it but can't free yourself in time. You keep struggling until you no longer have any strength.

Why would Henry attack you? It's a question you take with you to your watery grave.

THE END

To follow another path, turn to page 11.
To learn more about the Knights Templar,
turn to page 101.

Heading toward the sewer doesn't seem like a great idea. Instead, you continue straight down the dark tunnel.

The passageway twists and turns. Finally, you see something reflecting your light against a wall in the distance. You rush toward it and find a tiny gold coin. You tug at it, and it slides out of the stone.

You examine the coin closely under your phone's light. On its front is the cross of the Knights Templar. This is the evidence you were looking for. The Templars indeed came to this very spot. Their legendary treasure could be right around the corner.

"That's far enough," says Henry from behind you.

You shine your light at Henry. There's something reflective in his hand as well. You study it. It's a Danish police badge.

"Let's head back topside, shall we?" he says. "I'd like to talk to you about vandalizing private property."

You sigh, but don't put up a fight.

Luckily, you don't spend the night in a jail cell. After paying a hefty fine, you're sent on your way home. On the plane, you pull the gold coin from your pocket. You managed to hide it from Henry and the other policemen. It's not the treasure you were after, but it is proof. That will have to do for now.

THE END

To follow another path, turn to page 11.
To learn more about the Knights Templar,
turn to page 101.

With the old book secured in your jacket pocket, you hurry down through the crack in the floor and out of the cave. You carefully jump for the handholds on the jutting rock. Luck is on your side once again. Your hands dig into the indentations, and your grip holds.

Ocean waves crash against the cliffs by the Lion's Head and Camel's Head rock formations at Bornholm.

You swing yourself over to the narrow ledge. It takes longer this time around to scoot back up the cliff. The mist from the ocean makes the ledge slippery and more dangerous.

Finally, you make it to the cliff's grassy top. You're tired, so you collapse to the ground. You think about the book and reach into your pocket for it. But when you pull it out and open it, the pages crumble in your hands. You found the treasure of the Knights Templar, but age and the fresh ocean air have hidden its secrets forever.

THE END

To follow another path, turn to page 11.
To learn more about the Knights Templar,
turn to page 101.

You know you need to get a record of this amazing find. With practiced skill and care, you gently open the book and snap a photo. You slowly and carefully turn the page and take another photo. You repeat this process until you've captured the entire book in your phone's memory.

Then you place the book in your jacket pocket. Right away, you feel its pages loosen from its spine. You're glad you took the time to preserve the information when you did. You're not sure if the book will survive the trip back to the top of the cliff.

Unfortunately, taking all those pictures took much longer than you expected. More than an hour has passed by the time you squeeze back down through the crack in the chamber's floor.

When you land in the cave tunnel below, your feet splash into three inches of sea water. With every step you take, the water gets deeper. The tide is coming in. And it's coming in fast.

You make it halfway down the tunnel before a large wave floods the entire cave. You feel yourself battered against the nearby wall. The water doesn't drain from the cave until the following morning. Unfortunately for you, that is much too late.

THE END

To follow another path, turn to page 11.
To learn more about the Knights Templar,
turn to page 101.

The Ark of the Covenant was a holy artifact for the Jewish people. It was kept in the Temple of Solomon in Jerusalem. The Ark disappeared after the temple was destroyed in 587 BCE.

CHAPTER 5

THE TRUTH BEHIND THE FICTION

The stories of the secret treasures of the Knights Templar are very compelling. These myths have found their way into several popular movies and novels such as *Indiana Jones and the Last Crusade* and *The Da Vinci Code*. Unfortunately, the legends of the Templars hiding treasures around the globe are mostly just that—legends.

There are many stories that say the Knights Templar guarded lost treasures that were found in Solomon's Temple. This religious building was said to house the fabled Ark of the Covenant. The Ark was a special golden box said to hold the remains of the original stone tablets inscribed with the Ten Commandments.

This myth began when the Templars set up a base at the site of the destroyed temple. Some believe that the Templars explored the site and found the Ark and perhaps other valuable artifacts.

Another legend says that the Templars were special guards of the Holy Grail. According to Christian scripture, Jesus drank from the Grail during his famous Last Supper.

The Templars were also said to possess a fragment of wood that was part of the "true cross" that Jesus was crucified on. It's thought that the Templars may have kept these prized treasures hidden along with gold and other valuables.

There is little evidence to back up the myths. However, many clues have been discovered over the years. Some secrets may be hidden in the walls of ancient churches. And the famous Templar cross has been found engraved on rocks and structures all over the world.

The Convent of Christ castle in Tomar, Portugal, was originally built as a stronghold by the Knights Templar in the 1100s CE.

Just what is fact and what is fiction? There is little historical proof to link the Holy Grail to the Knights Templar. Instead, this holy relic is most likely a product of fiction. It's famous due to mythical stories about King Arthur and his knights.

The voyage of Henry Sinclair is also questionable. Sinclair is rumored to have traveled to North America years before Christopher Columbus. Some say he hid the Knights Templar treasures during this trip.

The evidence of Sinclair's voyage supposedly comes from letters that were misinterpreted over the years. In fact, the letters may not have even existed in the first place. Many historians who've written about Sinclair fail to mention any journeys he took to the New World.

Some people feel that the mysterious order of the Knights Templar continues on to this day. They think that the group evolved into the Freemasons or other secret societies. It's often said that truth is stranger than fiction. But in this case, the opposite is probably true. When the Knights Templar were disbanded by King Philip IV, the organization likely came to a complete end.

If the Knights Templar did hide any treasure, it has yet to be found. Their true legacy lies more in our imaginations than in history books. That's probably why these famous knights continue to fascinate us to this day.

WHERE IS THE TEMPLAR TREASURE?

Over the years, there have been many rumored locations of the Knights Templar treasures. This map of the world shows many of the spots that have attracted treasure hunters for centuries.

OAK ISLAND, NOVA SCOTIA
The famed Money Pit on Canada's Oak Island has long been rumored to hold Templar gold.

WESTFORD, MASSACHUSETTS
The Westford Knight sculpture may have links to Templar lore.

NEWPORT, RHODE ISLAND
Legends connect the circular Newport Tower to Scottish Templar Knights.

BORNHOLM, DENMARK
Stone structures and circular
churches on this island pose
interesting Templar mysteries.

ROSLIN, MIDLOTHIAN, SCOTLAND
The Rosslyn Chapel is
rumored to have housed
Templar survivors after the
order was dissolved.

DARVEL, EAST AYRSHIRE, SCOTLAND
The Knights Templar were once
granted lands in this mysterious town.

OTHER PATHS TO EXPLORE

>>> The European headquarters of the Knights Templar was once located in France. While their impressive fortress no longer remains, tourists can still enjoy Templar tours that recount the order's long history. Imagine hunting for the Templars' treasure in modern-day Paris. How would you try to unlock their long-hidden mysteries? Would you start in religious buildings? Could answers lurk in sewers or tunnels underground?

>>> On Oak Island in Nova Scotia, Canada, many believe the Knights Templar created the fabled Money Pit. It's thought to be a layered treasure vault built with secret booby traps. These traps include channels that filled rapidly with ocean water. Imagine you're searching for the Templars' treasure on Oak Island. How would you dig up a treasure that was buried underwater? What modern methods could help you in your quest?

>>> Many believe that the hidden treasures of the Knights Templar have been passed down to modern-day secret societies. Imagine joining an organization similar to the Freemasons. If you became a loyal member of this group, how would you discover information on the Knights Templar? What would you do with the information once you uncovered it?

BIBLIOGRAPHY

BBC.com.uk: *From Jerusalem to Rosslyn?: The Templars in Scotland.* https://www.bbc.co.uk/legacies/myths_legends/scotland/lothian/article_1.shtml

Haagensen, Erling, and Henry Lincoln. *The Templars Secret Island: The Knights, the Priest and the Treasure.* Moreton-in-Marsh, UK: Windrush, 2000.

Jones, Dan. *The Templars: The Rise and Spectacular Fall of God's Holy Warriors.* New York: Viking, 2017.

Rosslyn Chapel.com: *History.* https://www.rosslynchapel.com/about/history/

Sora, Steven. *The Lost Treasure of the Knights Templar: Solving the Oak Island Mystery.* Rochester, Vermont: Destiny Books, 1999.

Wasserman, James. *An Illustrated History of the Knights Templar.* Rochester, Vermont: Destiny Books, 2006.

GLOSSARY

authorities (uh-THAWR-uh-tees)—people who have control or power over others in a given situation

avalanche (AV-uh-lanch)—a large mass of snow, ice, rock, or other material that suddenly slides down the side of a mountain

crucify (KROO-suh-fahy)—to put to death by nailing or binding someone to a cross

curator (KYOOR-ay-tuhr)—a person in charge of a museum, art collection, or other valuable items

disintegrate (dis-IN-tuh-grayt)—to break up into small parts as the result of decay

inscription (in-SKRIP-shuhn)—writing or carving of words on wood or metal

mausoleum (maw-suh-LEE-uhm)—a large building that holds tombs

medieval (mee-DEE-vuhl)—having to do with the period of history between 500 and 1450 CE

runes (ROONS)—mysterious marks or letters that are carved into wood or stone

scaffolding (SKAH-fuhl-ding)—a temporary framework or set of platforms used to support people and materials while working on a building

READ MORE

Baby Professor. *Knights Templar: The Fellow-Soldiers of Christ.* Newark, DE: Speedy Publishing, LLC, 2017.

Fabiny, Sarah. *What Are Castles and Knights?* New York: Penguin Workshop, 2022.

Hoena, Blake. *Medieval Knights: Europe's Fearsome Armored Soldiers.* North Mankato, MN: Capstone Press, 2019.

INTERNET SITES

10 Reasons the Knights Templar Were History's Fiercest Fighters
history.com/news/knights-templar-facts-crusades-wealth

Knights Templar
worldhistory.org/Knights_Templar/

Where Did the Templar Treasure Go?
history.co.uk/shows/lost-relics-of-the-knights-templar/articles/where-did-the-templar-treasure-go

ABOUT THE AUTHOR

Author photo courtesy of Dorothy Manning Photography.

Matthew K. Manning is the author of more than 100 books and dozens of comic books. Some of his favorite projects include the popular comic book crossover *Batman/Teenage Mutant Ninja Turtles Adventures* and the 12-issue series *Marvel Action: Avengers* for IDW, *Exploring Gotham City* for Insight Editions, and the six-volume chapter book series *Xander and the Rainbow-Barfing Unicorns* for Capstone. Manning lives in Asheville, North Carolina, with his wife Dorothy and their two daughters, Lillian and Gwendolyn. Visit him online at www.matthewkmanning.com.